THE STORY
OF SELBORNE

and

The Cult of the
English Countryside

by

ARTHUR STOWELL

Published by
Stobooks

First published 2003

by

Stobooks

1 Riverside Cottages, The Dean,

Alresford, Hampshire SO24 9BE

In association with

The Gilbert White Museum and Oates Memorial Library

Arthur Stowell

ISBN: 0-9544798-0-7

Contents

Appendices

Acknowledgements

In attempting to write a history of a place from the earliest times to the present day, inevitably one needs a great deal of help from people with specialised knowledge of sources for the many periods of archaeology and history .

The Local Studies Department of the Hampshire County Library Service has, as always, been helpful. Similarly the Hampshire Record Office staff are always patient and willing to help.

In Selborne I have had much assistance from the Staff of the Gilbert White Museum and from Lord Selborne and Natalie Mees.

I have gathered much factual information from the Selborne Association Newsletters especially the numerous historical articles by Dr. E.M. Yates.

Many of the illustrations are by the kind permission of the Hampshire County Council Museum Service and from Chrispics collection of photographs of Selborne – Brian Wynne has again provided a delightful, imaginative cover.

My greatest thanks are to my wife Win for typing my most difficult script.

It is, of course, the author's responsibility for the facts and their interpretation as well as for any errors or omissions.

Introduction

M any writers of fiction begin with the disclaimer that none of the characters bear any relationship to anyone living or dead. The writer of history has to do the opposite – his characters are all dead but they once were living and the landscape and places in which they lived are still there, somewhat modified perhaps in various way – a hill is still a hill and a stream is probably still running.

There have been many books written about Selborne, a village in East Hampshire, mostly concentrating on the life and writings of the Reverent Gilbert White who spent much of his life there. He lived from 1720 till 1793 in what we call the Age of Enlightenment in the reigns of George II and George III. He wrote mostly as a keen observer of natural history and the wildlife which was all around him in his quiet village. The letters which he wrote were compiled into the NATURAL HISTORY of SELBORNE and have been printed over and over again. He also wrote a GARDEN KALENDAR and something of the ANTIQUITIES of SELBORNE.

This book however is not a biography of Gilbert White nor an examination of his writings, for this has been done by many writers notably most recently by Richard Mabey in 1986 in his GILBERT WHITE a biography of the author of the NATURAL HISTORY of SELBORNE.

The sub-title of this work is the Cult of the English Countryside looking at the ways in which the countryside has fascinated so many people who live mainly in towns and cities and regarded it, including Selborne as an idyllic place.

Up to the beginning of the Industrial Revolution in the middle of the eighteenth century – roughly speaking Gilberts White's lifetime – virtually everywhere in Britain was countryside. There were very few large towns or cities, London, Bristol, Norwich, and even in London there were fragments of rural areas embedded in it with names such as St. Martins in the Fields, Smithfield, Stepney Green or Hackney Marshes.

These chapters will attempt to outline a little of the history and pre-history of Selborne and to see how this area of Hampshire looked to people who lived outside it and how our mainly urban population today view it as an idyllic place.

The people living in Selborne today, some born here, some recent immigrants and some short time residents may find history helps them to feel a sense of belonging although it has to be more than nostalgia for the past.

The village is not of course, always idyllic!!

It has a busy road for its main street with traffic a danger to humans and animals, with vehicles emitting noxious fumes and gases plus noise undreamt of a hundred years ago apart from the odd traction engine. One can get away from this on foot in peace especially if the mobile phone is left at home.

Selborne from the Hanger

A.K.Stowell

Chapter 1

The Archaeologist's Story

T he archaeologist is working as if with a jigsaw puzzle with most of the pieces missing and possibly several jigsaw sets all mixed up. The only whole piece is the jigsaw box which represents the landscape much as we see it today. The hills and valleys, heathlands, bogs, rivers and streams as well as woods and forests of which there are only scattered remains today.

The long range of chalk hills known as the South Downs, with narrow gaps and breaks, cross the whole of Southern England roughly parallel with the south coast with their highest point about 800ft above sea level.

The village of Selborne lies in the lea of a part of this system of chalk hills, below a hill called Selborne Hill whose steep northen slopes are known as the Hangers. the story of who lived in this area and when, has yet to be unravelled by the archaeologist looking at earlier times, then the historian working with written records carries on the story.

There are traces of people living in the Selborne area, perhaps, ten thousand years ago, probably nomadic families having no permenant place to stay. Archoeologists called these people Mesolithic or Middle Stone Age. Evidence of there temporary camps usually with tiny stone chipped tools, have been found on the light sandy soils to the north of Selborne at Oakhanger and Short Heath. They would probably have had the cults of their ancestors or magic connections with their hunting, fishing and plant gathering, unfortunately we have no idea of the size of their populations.

After the passage of several thousand years the first farmers appeared on our island. About five thousand years ago farming began with either new people from Europe or possibly just with new ideas passed on to the existing population. or indeed both happening together. Archaeologists called them Neolithic or New Stone Age people. They cleared much of the forests and wild wood.

Farming necessitates staying in one place for at least a reasonable period of time in farmsteads or hamlets, although they probably still did much hunting of wild deer, boar and birds. The growing of corn had first been developed in the Middle East as well as the domestication of animals, sheep, pigs, cattle and a dog to guard them.

Their finely polished stone tools haave been found in various places in Selborne. Their burial places – long barrows – some are still visible today especialy in Wiltshire and Salisbury Plain. It is in the western areas of Britain that we can speculate on the cults which have left the great stone circles at Avebury and Stonehenge also "woodhenges" uncovered by archaeologists. All of these seem to have required the expenditure of vast amounts of labour from presumably a sizeable population. Less spectacular is the discovery by pollen analysis, that grasslands of this period contained many of the meadow plants which we find today such as ox-eyed daisy, marjoram and many more known to Gilbert White.

A new technology, the use of metal was to arrive from continental Europe either by new people or by learned technology and almost certainly by itinerant metal smiths. First was the use of copper to make tools while still using flint tips for arrows. A harder metal was made by smelting tin with copper to make bronze. Much tin was mined in Cornwall and copper in the western mountains of Britain, the bronze tools and weapons were much in demand.

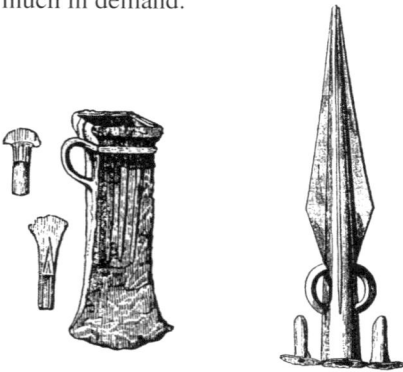

Bronze Age socketed axe and spear

Selborne farmers and chieftains clearly had its bronze age, shown by the discovery of a hoard of swords, spearheads and axes probably belonging to a travelling smith. Evidence of where people lived can be seen in the many round barrows, marked on our maps as "tumuli", the burial places of the more important members of the community. A number of bronze age barrows can still be seen in the Selborne area, one at Blackmoor, another at The Warren, also at Worldham although many must have disappeared as the result of ploughing for two or three thousand years. The cult of the dead ancestors and their re-living in another world required that their burial should be accompanied with pots of food and their favourite weapons, bracelets or torques.

By about 700 BC iron was beginning to take the place of bronze, it was cheaper and the raw materials was more easily available in much of

Britain. It's use may signal the arrival in Britain of Celtic people from continental Europe. They farmed extensively, especially on the lighter soils, some Iron Age remains have been found at Oakhanger near Selborne. There seems to have been a marked increase in population during the Iron Age which was a very long one. The various chieftains or kingdoms seemed to have feared invasion of their territory since with much labour they turned many hill tops into fortified areas which occur in many parts of Hampshire. Near to Selborne is Old Winchester Hill with it's hill top fort; others are at Winchester, St. Catherines Hill and Danebury in the west of the county.

The large number of farms and hamlets were undoubtedly connected by many footpaths and lanes, many of which are the basis of our present road system. By about 200BC these Iron Age people were influenced by Roman Europe. They were using money as a means of exchange and the "finds" of coins brings us to the beginnings of "history", for they show that the kingdom of thee Atrebates, which Julius Caesar mentions, stretched over much of Hampshire and West Sussex including the area now called Selborne.

It was the Iron Age Britain which the Romans invaded in 43AD; Julus Caesar had nearly raided in 55 and 54BC. After 43BC they stayed on for nearly 400 years – at least a dozen generations. They brought an urban civilization which they imposed on the old Iron Age patterns of farmsteads and fields. The Romans built towns and linked them with long straight roads. Chichester was near the coast not far from the Selborne area, with Winchester a few miles to the west and Silchester a town of 100 acres a few score miles to the north.

Roads linking these towns passed close to the east of where Selborne now is.

A large number of Roman coins were found at Blackmoor, possibly the contents of a pay chest from the time of Allectus in the third century. A Roman cremation site has also been found at Blackmoor. The names of Wick Hill and Wickwood may retain the Roman (Latin) word vicus meaning a row of houses or a hamlet. There are several sites of villas which were large farms or estates between

Selborne and Winchester possibly occupied by Romanised Britons or former chiefs. At Alice Holt there were also a number of potteries possibly supplying the large town of Calleva (Silchester).

The theme of this book is the cult of the countryside, largely by town dwellers looking perhaps with envy at the idealised countryside. Long before the Romans invaded Britain they had a great concern for the countryside; in the second century BC a Roman writer named Cato had written a treatise called "De Agriculturae" – concerning Agriculture and Virgil wrote his four books "The Georgies" celebrating all that was good in the countryside; he lived much the same time as Julius Caesar. These writings were to be studied by classical scholars in Britain from the sixteenth to the twentieth centuries.

The Romans had a word for leisure – "otium" with an ideal of peaceful life in rural estates with villas, gardens and orchards. How much these ideals were transfered to Romans or Romanised Britons in the villas of Hampshire we can only speculate.

The Roman occupation of Britain had many ups and downs but finally came to an end in 410 AD when the last Roman legions left to defend Rome from attacks by "barbarians". Some villas were already derelict but the town of Silchester seems to have been occupied well into the fifth century. How long and what happened to Romanised Britons who farmed in the Selborne area we must leave to more archaeology to uncover.

The archaeologist's story continues but with very little and sometimes contradictory evidence; historians call the post Roman period "The Dark Ages" which gradually develops into Anglo Saxon England, over a long period of time, a length of time much the same as that of the Iron Age. People went on having babies and dying and sometimes leaving their homes such as those Britains who moved to a part of Gaul, now called Brittany.

People were moving into the British Isles as well as moving out. The newcomers known to historians as Angles Saxons and Jutes brought with them a new language which largely replaced the old Celtic and which would be the forerunner of modern English. The very name of Selborne derives from "selle" – a willow or sallow tree and "borne" a shady swift flowing stream. For the Anglo Saxons a shady or muddy stream was called a brook; their word for a steep-sided wooded hill has become Hanger – a familiar part of Selborne.

An unanswerable question might be how far the memory of the people of Selborne stretched back to life in Roman times; there were very little if any to contemplate as there were in Colchester or Lincoln. Christianity which had had a place in Roman Britian – whose British bishops in 314AD attended the council of Arles in Provence seems to have withered away until in 597 St. Augustine brought his Christian mission to Canterbury in Kent. The language of the Christian church was Latin, a legacy from the Roman Empire. Literacy increased so that written evidence for Anglo Saxon England exists mainly in charters of land, mainly connected with the Church. Many hamlets and farmsteads grew into villages dominated by a church building and with recognisable names such as Selborne. Churches had saints names and the cult of the saint often became the identifying feature of the place for many of the inhabitants. The church was to become a powerful institution which persisted as a form of local government and control right through the Anglo Saxon period . In Hartley (Hartely Mauditt) and Headley, the "ley" element comes from "leah" meaning a clearing in a wood – land or meadow; Newton (Newton Valence) just means new farm; the "don" in Farringdon indicates a flat top hill. The Manditt and Valence parts of the names are just family names – more about these in another chapter. There are however some names surviving from the Celtic past, mostly river names such as Meon, Itchen, Test, Avon and Candover.

The conversion of England to Christianity after 597 and of Hampshire – Wessex – after 634 when Birinus was its first missionary and bishop, has produced less archaeological evidence. Christians were buried with usually, no grave goods and not cremated as pagans had been. The archaeologist can however study several late Saxon church buildings, the nearest to Selboure being Corhampton in the Meon Valley where the whole but small church has survived. Winchester, not far away, was to be the centre of much history, ecclesiastical, art and royal happenings until it was overtaken by London.

The archaecologists story does not finish here since the mediaeval countryside has left the traces in and under the soil with field systems and deserted villages.

Chapter 2

"1066 and all that"

We have had to invent names for various periods of history in order to make manageable the passing of years and centuries. The time between the coming of the Normans in 1066, a date remembered by most people, up to the beginning of the time of the Tudor kings and queens, we call The Middle Ages or Mediaeval period, a label not used before the early seventeenth century. The period is more than four hundred years in length and some five hundred years before our present time. It is characterised by a relatively slow rate of change in society and economic life but with sometimes violent changes of government. Perhaps the most important aspect of life was that of religion – Christianity and the christian church were to effect everybody from all stratas of society from the King down to the humblest serf. Geographically the idea of Europe hardly existed but that of Christendom was a firm concept.

The Norman Conquest of England in1066 after the battle of Hastings by Duke William of Normandy was to cause considerable and violent changes to England. When he conquered Anglo Saxon England with a relatively small number of lords and knights he divided up the land with its various manors, he had some for himself, some for the church and others for supporting Norman knights none of whom had large blocks of land so that none could be over-mighty. Selborne church was given to the monastery of St. Michael in Normandy. In the years after the conquest many Frenchmen from other parts of France came to settle in Britain.

Twenty years after the main invasion William began a grand inventory of his land, it was called the Domesday Book and the survey was based on Winchester. It gives us written evidence of most of the villages, manors and the names of those who held the land, including Selborne. Clerks went out from place to place getting evidence from the local people. The books tell us that Selborne manor, a word not frequently used, was king's land and that Queen Edith held it——it does not mean that she lived here but that she had the income derived from it. Since it was royal it never paid tax but the king gave half a hide of land with the church to someone named Radfred the priest——our first Selborne citizen known by name. The Domesday Book tells us that before 1066 it was valued at 12s 6d and that now (ie at 1086) it was only 8s 4d so it had gone down in value as had many other places. Another entry under the heading of Neatham Hundred one of the divisions of the shire, says that Walter son of Roger held Selborne and Herbert from him—— so we know the names of a more of our early inhabitants. Also that Alfward, held from the last Anglo Saxon King Edward the Confessor in freehold; then and now (1086) it answered for four hides and that it had land for two ploughs and owned one plough; there were four villagers and two small holders with two ploughs and two slaves (serfs). There was an acre of meadow and enough woodland to feed three pigs and it's value before 1066 was 60s, later 40s but now 70s, so it had gone up in value. We have then, a somewhat confused idea of the manors that made up Selborne. The eight men mentioned probably had eight families of perhaps five or six people so the village of Selborne would have had about fifty people living in the vicinity of the church and the square green called Plestor where they could hold a market and gather on saints days.

In addition to the village there were hamlets or manors at Norton, Blackmoor, and Oakhanger. The boundries of Selborne had probably remained unchanged since earlier Anglo Saxon times based mainly on the geology of the chalk escarpment and the more fertile marlstone. As in many parts of lowland Britain, the people of Selborne worked a three field system, using large open fields divided into strips and rotating their crops over a three year period of wheat, barley or oats and one left fallow, unplanted for animals to graze and manure. The names of the three open fields were King's Field, North Field and the third covering the Ewell and the Park, which villagers cultivated, the strips were decided each year at the Manoral Court. After the harvest was gathered their animals wandered over the stubble looked after by young people, perhaps the origin of some of our nursery rhymes such as Little Boy Blue or Goose Girl. The use of open fields with strips continued until the enclosures of the early nineteenth century, although some enclosures had been made since Tudor times causing a good deal of rural poverty. The enclosures produced fields with hedges which we see today as part of our historic countryside although in many parts of England they are relatively recent.

It is noticible that most people, including the clergy have only one name – Radfred, Mathew or Alfward but by 1221 a Philip has a second name "de Lucy derived from his original home, similarly Gilbert de Bohunt; not until the fourteenth century were surnames common sometimes related to their place of birth, or their occupation or their physical characteristics such as Long, Brown, White.

There are examples in Selborne and it's area, thus Richard de Norton in the twelfth century taking his name from that hamlet and giving rise in the fourteenth century to two separate families of that name appearing in the Subsidy Roll – a kind of tax list, one of these families was to persist in Tisted for several hundred years, indeed the name Norton appears in quite large numbers in our modern telephone directory.

Another of these richer famlies in Selborne were the Gurdons, Norman originally but soon to lose their Frenchness and become Englishmen. Adam de Gurdon's name first appears in Selborne in 1206, during the reign of King John and probably given the manor for his military efforts. Several Gurdon's followed until a John Gurdon's name appears in the 1327 Sibsidy List, taxed for his lands in Selborne and Tisted; soon after this the lands passed to the female side of the family and the name was lost.

The Gurdons were to become of the benefactors of Selborne Priory whose founder was Peter des Roches a name more important in England than the Nortons or the Gurdons.

Chapter 3

Religion, Religion and Religion

R eligion was almost the politics of the time, affecting peoples lives at all levels but in different ways. Peter des Roches came from Poitou in central France arriving in England in 1200 and quickly rose to prominence. He became Bishop of Winchester, an immensely important and rich position in the kingdom. He supported King John when he was excommunicated by the Pope, later becoming tutor to the King's son Henry who he crowned King as Henry III in 1216 after John's death. Peter later went on a crusade between 1227 and 1231 and when he returned he founded a priory in Selborne dedicated to the Blessed Virgin Mary. He endowered it with newly purchased lands including the manor of Selborne amounting to several thousand acres, the charter of the priory was dated the 4th May 1233.

The priory was of the Augustinian Order for fourteen Black Canons who were secular priests – they were ordained, which most monks were not. The Augustinian Order already had a number of other priories in Hampshire Southampton founded in 1127, Mottisfont in 1201 as well as Christchurch and Portchester. King Henry I first introduced the order to England in about 1106, so Selborne was a late foundation.

Stone had been quarried in Selborne since at least 1222 and was used at Winchester Castle and Titchfield Abbey. The names of some of the builders of the priory have survived, there was Stephen le Mazon who was the master mason and Richard Cementarious who had both worked previously for King Henry III and Bishop de Roches.

In 1233 James de Norton, whose family has already been mentioned and James de Ochanger and King Henry III did likewise. Bishop, Peter des Roches gave to the priory, the churches of Selborne, Oakhanger and Blackmoor which had previously belonged to the abbey of Mont St. Michel in Normandy, some of these may have been mere chapels but would have had some land.

The priory put Selborne on the map, so to speak, although there were no maps at that time. In May 1236 Richard Duke of Cornwall who was Henry III's brother, stayed there on his way to a crusade in Syria. The double headed eagle which was the badge of the Duke of Cornwall, is to be seen on the floor tiles both at Selborne and Titchfield.

The priory was financed by various other means such as by people seeking merit for their souls. Some were tiny legacies like one penny per year from Alice de Therdene, another where Hugh and Maud de Bromdene in 1236 gave land in exchange for supplies of bread and wine for the rest of their lives – a sort of old age pension. The priory also had land at West Tisted encumbered with debt which they were still repaying two hundred years later!

In 1270 Henry III granted to the priory a market every Tuesday and a fair on the Feast of the Assumption (14 - 16th August) held on Selborne Plestor which had been given to the village by Sir Adam de Gurdon.

King Edward I visited the priory at least twice but the priory seems to have been in increasing financial trouble; it was excused fines because of claims of poverty. In 1322 in the reign of Edward II the priory, like many other priors and abbots was ordered to raise men-at-arms to muster at Coventry in order to march against the rebel army of the Earl of Leicester – were these young men from Selborne or paid soldiers from the area?

The fourteenth century was one of disasters, one following the other. In 1315 and 1317 heavy summer rains caused failure of crops which led to famine throughout much of Europe. Within less than a generation the so called the Hundred YearsWar with France began making a drain on English manpower. Then in 1348 and 9 came the widespread bubonic plague – The Black Death – coming from Europe first to Dorset, then to other towns on the south coast. There can be little doubt that Selborne and it's priory could have suffered many deaths as well as economic disruption. The fear of death, and hell which might follow, was constant with mediaeval people. The high and sudden mortality from plague must have increased this fear.

After 1349 the severity of the plague decreased but outbreaks occured for the next two centuries. In 1381 came the Peasants Revolt partly caused by the imposition of a Poll Tax. A few years before the prior had to be forgiven by Edward III for money which the priory owed – it seems to have been in general decline. although the King still visited and stayed at Selborne.

William of Wykeham, bishop of Winchester, criticised the priory for several shortcomings – the brethren must learn to read properly, they must not wear coloured shoes or stockings, no fur edged clothes or gloves and, worst of all they must not pawn the priory's valuables or books.

The finances of the priory gradually got worse and by the 1400s only four canons and their servants were left. The prior, Peter Berne resigned and the bishop replaced him with Thomas Fairwise from Lancashire – a long way from Selborne. By now other Augustine Priories in Hampshire were poor, among them Southhampton and St. Cross Winchester.

Magdalen College Tower

Bishop Waynflete finally gave Selborne Priory and all its lands and property to the newly formed Magdalen College Oxford. the only canon by this time was Thomas Ashford aged 72, the Pope confirmed the closing in June 1486 just 250 years after its founding. Thomas Ashford was given a pension of £6-13s-4d a year for life.

We may ask what effect there was for Selborne having both a parish church and a priory both dedicated to the Virgin Mary. It was probably important for the women of the village for the Virgin was their special saint with a chapel and altar within the church especially for them.

Mediaeval people worked hard from dawn to dusk and virtually the only allevation of this toil was the many religious festivals, holy days and saints days which formed the calender of the year round which all life revolved. Rents were paid on Lady Day (25th March) or Michaelmas (29th September). Some festivals were fixed Christmas Day 25th December, Epiphany the 6th January and on 2nd Febuary was Candlemas, the Purification of the Virgin Mary when candles were taken home to protect against sickness or sudden death. It was also the day when Judas was allowed out of hell for one day!

The 25th March was the festival of the annunciation of the Virgin Mary and also the beginning of the New Year. Hallowmas or All Saints Day was the 1st November preceded by All Hallow E'en when ghosts and evil spirits were about. All these festivals were very real to people of the middle Ages. The other major feasts such as Good Friday, Easter Day and Whitsun were moveable dates depending,on an Easter Table of dates which incidentally has provided historians with the dates of other happenings.

Both the priory and the church promoted the cult of the Virgin Mary and the priory claimed to possess the little finger bone of St. John the Baptist as well as a a piece of bone of St. Richard of Chichester. The former bone was most unlikely but the latter quite possible since Richard bishop of Chichester had visited the priory in 1250 and had been a friend of the first prior. The uncertainties of life in mediaeval times, of famine, plague and warfare would have made people cling to religion, the church taught them how the saints and even their bodily parts, could intercede for their souls. It applied just as much to the poor men and women as to those who could afford to pay for charities and priests to pray for them after they died.

With the closing of the priory in 1486 this devotion had to be deflected elsewhere by the Reformation of the church in the Tudor sixteenth century. Selborne apparently a remote and small village, became well known for its priory and the comings and goings of Kings and Bishops. In addition at

ACM905.1.622

ACM905.1.622 Temple Farm, from a drawing by S. H. Grimson (?)
(1733-1794) – 1766

Southerington, not far from the village, was a property of the Knights Templars – crusading knights, called a "preceptory" which undoubtedly had many visitors. The name Temple still survives on modern maps. The Grange or great barn is in Selborne Village a mile away from the priory so there would have been frequent contacts between village people and the priory, a pleasant enough walk in spring or summer but intensely dark in winter. Despite their religion people were frightened by all sorts of devils – after all they had seen them painted on the walls of their church. There were also other creatures such as the Green Man lurking in the trees as well as Hern the Hunter, Jack O'Lantern or Will of the Wisp and assorted fairies.

Present day people have rarely experienced such intense winter darkness except for a few years in the Second World War when the enforced "blackout" made outdoor travel often dangerous and frightening. The mediaeval darkness was in cottages and sheds as well as out of doors, with shadows thrown from glowing fire-light——there were robbers as well as ghosts to be talked about. We may see, in our mind's eye, the ghosts of those canons, young and old, who walked down the path to the Plestor, the Church or the Grange Did they secretly meet some village girl in the Lythe?

1337.—Female Costume in the time of Henry V. (Royal MS. D 3.)

Chapter 4

The Tudor Legacy

T he period of the Tudor Kings and Queens lasted just over one hundred
years, three or four generations beginning with the defeat of Richard
III at the Battle of Bosworth in 1485 and a year before the final closing of
Selborne priory, when Henry Tudor became King Henry VIII. The period
finished with the death of the unmarried Queen Elizabeth in 1603. We all
know of Henry VIII and his six wives and his closing down of the
monasteries but Selborne's Priory was closed a couple of generations
previously and its land and income transferred to Magdalen College Oxford.
Selborne Priory building was almost certainly used as a quarry for its fine
stone so soon became a ruin.

The parish church survived from its mediaeval past – it is still there
and used as a place of Christian worship which would not be understood
by its mediaeval men and women. The inside of the church was changed in
the Tudor times out of all recognition. The statue of the Virgin and Child
had disappeared and so had the brightly painted one of its early bishop
Peter des Roches, perhaps there had been another of Bishop Waynflete.
The angels had literally flown away and the brightly painted rood screen
with its crucified Christ had been pulled down, the whole church had been
whitewashed covering up the wall painting of St. Christopher and the

dreadful "Doom" with its demons torturing the souls of the departed – us the villagers! For some reason the painting on the walls of St. Boltolphs at Hardham in West Sussex have survived so we know something of their mediaeval message. These changes were the result of the Tudor Church Reformation. The mid-Tudor parish church was much lighter but less awe-inspiring than the candle lit statues and wall pantings. Reading was much easier, the printed Bible and Prayer book was the keystone of Reformation.

Gutenberg had invented the printing press at Mainz in Germany in the 1450s, and the invention had spread to London by 1477. Within a few years the Bible and religious books so carefully copied by the canons and monks were no longer in use, their place being taken by printed versions in large numbers. What is more, they were in English not Latin. Selborne's Latin Bible, the Vulgate, which only the priest and perhaps a few parishioners could read, had been replaced by an English version on a lectern at the junction of the choir and nave. This "Byble in Englyshe" first appeared in 1539 and was known as the Great Bible authorised by Henry VIII himself, sometimes called Cranmer's Bible because he wrote a preface to it. How soon Selborne got its copy we do not know.

A new prayer book called the Book of Common Prayer produced by Archbishop Cranmer was published in 1549 in the new reign of the young King Edward VI and a second edition in 1552. The people of Selborne would have noticed that it retained the old Latin titles such as "Venite Exultemus Domino" but with words in English – "O come let us sing unto the Lord" and "Te Deum Laudamus", "We praise thee O God" as part of the Mattins or Morning Prayers. Similarly in the Evening Prayer the English verses begin "My soul doth magnify the Lord" with the Latin title "Magnificat" and the Nunc Dimittis" is the heading for "Lord now letest thou thy servant depart in peace."

Various bibles and revised prayer books came out in the reign of Elisabeth I as well as the very popular Foxes Book of Martyrs. It seems likely that many more people had learned to read by the second half of the sixteenth century; it was accepted that the gentry might read to their families but that the poor might get ideas above their station. Children were taught their catechisim by rote. By this time too, boys who had their first tonsure as acolytes or altar boys – shaving the hair from the top of the head – had forgotten what it was all about and had long since let their hair grow.

The Selborne church itself belonged to Magdalen College Oxford who appointed its vicars.

The people of Selborne went on having babies, getting married, and dying but now in the Tudor period of change, their names were written down in the Parish Registers beginning in 1538 by order of Thomas Cromwell who was chief minister of Henry VIII. The keeping of Parish Records was only one example of the State interfering in local affairs, much in the reign of Queen Elizabeth I. There were acts of parliament allowing local Justices of the Peace to imprison under the Bastardy Act and another act to suppress begging. Another act in 1581 made church attendance compulsory, poor old Elizabeth Tichborne, a Catholic, was fined for not so doing despite the fact she was bed-ridden. An earlier act in 1558, the Militia Act required even small villages to provide armed men, a kind of Home Guard; Selborne was to supply 29 archers and many "billmen" – virtually every able-bodied man. Alton had to supply many more. The inventory of the possessions of John Paulet of Norton one of the better off, included two steel coats, two bills, three sheaves of arrows, a sword and dagger.

Another order of Queen Elizabeth was that the boundaries of parishes should be confirmed by "beating the boundries", this was done at Selborne at Rogation Tide in May every few years until 1780 when it fell out of use because maps such as Milne's map of Hampshire 1791 were now fairly accurate. What we know least about our Tudor ancestors, or indeed our mediaeval ones, is their systems of belief, of there state of mind about religion and it's rituals, of their relationships with family, their fear of death and hell, as well as robbery and violence. How many people in Selborne still had belief in the Green Man in the woods or in Hern the Hunter or ghosts in general. Their horizons were limited, only a few went as far as Winchester or Chichester. Pilgrimages so popular in the middle ages were no longer in fashion; clergy no longer went to Rome or Avignon and by Tudor times "clerks" were no longer clergy.

A few of the better-off people in Selborne left wills and inventories of their goods, often few in number. Their real wealth lay in the land which they rented or occupied and the stock which they reared. As we have already seen, by this time, Magdalen College Oxford owned much of the former priory lands and therefore received the rents from them. Selborne had no large estates such as Basing or the Vine.

One of the Tudor wills left by Christopher Baker of Selborne tells us that he lived at Grange Farm about the year 1550, part of the old priory land and grange which was its main storage barn. His house consisted of a single-storey with a hall and a bedchamber and a kitchen, with out-houses where he kept his cart and plough. He also had five beehives or skips; there is no mention of horse or oxen for his plough but there was bacon in the kitchen, so he must have kept pigs. His moveable furniture and belongings were simple; the hall which was the main living room had a table top and two trestles, one form and five stools. The fireplace not being movable is not mentioned in the inventory; the bedchamber list shows only bedding so they may have slept on straw pallets on the floor. Clothes were of wool or linen and were kept in four coffers or chests – no wardrobes in this period but there were probably nails or hooks for hanging garments.

The kitchen may have been in a separate out-house, there were fire irons and spits for roasting. Also listed were brass vessels, probably cooking pots and pewter plates as well as wooden buckets or tubs. Spoons and drinking vessels were often made from cows' horns and therefore too cheap to be recorded.

A family named Baker – John, Roger and William were listed in a taxation list for Selborne in 1524 [Henry VIII's reign] so Christopher may have been the son of one of these. Roger the most wealthy had been assessed at £7 while John was assessed at 13 marks, a mark being an old coin valued at 13 shillings and 4 pence, ie. two thirds of a pound. The last son, William, was listed at 20 shillings (a shilling was until the 1960s a twentieth part of a pound or twelve pence)

The will and inventory of John Paulet of Norton was slightly different in that it listed seventeen milk cows and one bull as well as ploughs, harrows and corn stored in the barn but no mention of sheep so common in Selborne. In his house as well as the usual beds, coffers and a table were silver spoons and a silver salt cellar showing that the Paulets were considerably richer than most others in the Selborne area and were part of what we would call the county family of Paulet.

Of the domestic buildings in the Selborne area very few remained from the late mediaeval period although their sites were frequently re-used. The Wakes, the Reverend Gilbert White's home and now a museum has a Tudor core, all much changed and added to. It was originally called "Coopers" after the family who lived in it and then changed to "Wakes" for the same reason.

ACM905.1.625 Goleigh, nr Selborne, Hampshire – December 1938

Not far from Selborne, at Prior's Dean, still, exists a fine late mediaeval manor house called Goleigh possible built as an open hall in 1466 – a date supported by tree-ring dating or denrochonology. The prior in question was the prior of Southwark and its purpose was to support Winchester College. The manor house was remodelled during the civil war period but it's exposed beams are what are so often regarded as "Tudor style". This was copied extensively in the twentieth century by many builders as a departure from classical styles. Of couse they were nothing like Goleigh either in construction or interior, but they seemed to express some desire to escape to a time called "The Good Old Days".

Selborne seems always to have connections with the building industry. The Pipe Rolls(accounts) of the bishop of Winchester show a payment for a special cart to carry stone from Selborne, probably for his Wolvesley Palace in Winchester – the cart horses were costed at two pence plus two pence for food for the men. A hundred years later the Pipe Rolls show a payment to Thomas Glasyer of Selborne for "remaking anew the windows of the lord's chamber broken by a great wind with glass", and "brought for the same by piece work £ 2." but William Bagge (for) mending the iron work 2s 6d. So glazing for windows in Selborne must have been possible from an early date, if one could afford it! By the Tudor period many cottages were having casement windows with small diamond pieces of glass set in lead, although sash windows did not begin to be used until the end of the eighteenth century.

Despite having building stone available Selborne had its own brickworks, its still there! During Tudor times many houses had brick chimney stack inserted sometimes with back-to-back fireplaces and some incorporating a brick bread oven. In mediaeval times the smoke from a fire in the centre of the hall had to find its way through a louvre in the roof. When the brick chimneys were in place the hall often had a ceiling inserted thus providing an upstairs chamber bedroom.

The reign of Elizabeth I is sometimes called the time of the great re-build, for houses both large and small. However it was also a period when whole villages were disappearing: Hartley Manditt just north of Selborne is one such, it mediaeval church still stands, also its pond but, the rest of the village has disappeared. At Abbotstone near Alresford even the church has gone, leaving only an outline in the ground with mounds where the cottages once stood. Their demise is often attributed to the Black Death which may well have weakened their population, but their final deserting was more likely due to change in agriculture or ownership of land. The sixteenth century saw an increasing interest in the land of England, our French connections having been finally severed when Calais was lost. John Leyland, who had been to Oxford and spent some time in Paris wrote an Itinerary of England for Henry VIII admiring rivers, woods and mountains.

Christopher Saxton produced an atlas in 1579 showing each county including Hampshire. A few years later William Camden produced a great topographical work called "Britannia" which went into many editions even in his own lifetime. In about 1595 John Norden, a surveyor by profession produced a map of Hampshire. Another map by John Speed in 1611 mis-spells "Shelburn" but gets "Selbarn Hundred" nearly right; it also marks Hartley (M anditt). The proliferation of maps and guides for travellers at this time shows at least a recognition of the differences in the countryside if not an actual cult. Maps are essentially practical but writing in verse expresses enjoyment and Shakespeare's sonnets, often about love, see it in the context of spring flowers or 'shall I compare thee to a summers day?' Or in A Midsummer Night's Dream the idyllic linesread 'I know a bank whereon the wild thyme blows' the image of the countryside is ever present.

Chapter 5

The Commonwealth and After

We are gently sliding out of the sixteenth century into the seventeen, the Stuart period, which seems to divide into two separate parts. Shakespeare was still alive and the new King James Bible was on the lectern in Selborne church, but we still have another hundred years to go before we come to Gilbert White's birth in 1720.

The first half of the century lead up to a vicious Civil War which was to effect much of Hampshire. The conflict was between the Stuart King Charles I and his Parliament largely about taxation but also about religion with the King and his followers, Cavaliers, mainly supporting the Anglican Church while many Parliamentarians, Roundheads, were Puritans. Fighting then occurred round and about in Alton, in Farnham and Winchester. Basing House was beseiged and finally destroyed by the Parliamentary army. How far Selborne was affected by the campaign which led up to the Battle of Cheriton in 1644 it is difficult to say. The parliamentary forces were moving from east to west in order to re-capture Winchester which was Royalist. The two armies clashed at Cheriton Down and the Royalist army was defeated.

The family name of Norton, mentioned in an earlier chapter appears again with a Colonel Richard Norton commanding the Alton regiment of the Hampshire trained bands in which some Selborne names occur on the muster roll including Wake from which the present home takes it's name. Selborne paid only £1 towards the Muster Master's expenses; the men got eight pence per day. It is likely that Selborne would have had its horses, carts and cattle requisitioned by the Parliamentary army and its hay and fodder taken to feed the troop's horses as well as food for foot soldiers. It gave the opportunity for some people to make money since a Robert Phillips of Selborne was charged with selling horses he had stolen to the Royalists at Basing House. By 1649 King Charles I had been executed and England was to become a Commonwealth for a decade, a period of some austerity with the heavy hand of puritanism. In 1657 John Longworth, vicar of Selborne was deprived of his living presumably because he followed the teachings of the Archbishop Laud, a high Anglican. However he was re-instated in 1660 when the Commonwealth ended and his puritan predecessor John Ferror had to retire. During that period over one hundred clergy had lost their livings in Hampshire though most regained them with the Restoration of King Charles II. Many country estates were returned to their original owners but Selborne had no big country house or estate.

The second half of the seventeenth century, according to modern historians, saw a marked improvement in town life which, perhaps, made the difference between town and country more apparent. The period produced a number of interesting writers of diaries and travels. Samuel Pepys' diary is well known but he was essentially a townsman spending most of his time in London. He did visit Portsmouth more than once apparently enjoying the greenness of the Hampshire hills. On another occasion he visited Winchester when the King was staying at the Deanery.

Another diarist was John Evelyn who had travelled widely in France, Switzerland and Italy including Venice and was interested in urban culture but he wrote a book, of which he was very proud, entitled *"Sylvia"* about forest trees which he presented to the Royal Society. It was not so much about landscape as about the value of timber for shipbuilding.

Another writer of the seventeenth century was John Aubrey who lived in Wiltshire and Dorset and was interested in the antiquities of those counties including Stonehenge and Avebury. He lived mostly in London but said he would like to have lived in Bristol, a then up and coming city. He was looking from the city to the countryside with its strange antiquities. He also produced a series of biographies, called *Brief Lives,* of people who lived in this and the previous century. Included in his list of prominent people was John Ogilby the map maker, the first person to include the roads of the country in strip form. Alton, Farringdon and Priors Dean are all on his map but not Selborne!

Towards the end of the century a female traveller Celia Fiennes, rode around much of Southern England between 1685 and 1712 noting in her diary the landscape and countryside through which she went.

How some of us used to live in the seventeenth century

Chapter 6

Gilbert White's Century

T he life of the Reverend Gilbert White of Selborne covered most of the eighteenth Century. He was born in 1720 when George I was king and died in 1793 when George III was on the throne. It was Gilbert White's writing published towards the end of his life which made the name of Selborne well known to the reading public and helped to make people aware of the natural history and countryside of east Hampshire much of which is still recognisable today.

He was not the first to write about country things. John Ray, the son of an Essex blacksmith, had written extensively about birds, fish and above all plants. He belongs to the previous century and died in 1705. Charles Linnaeus born in Sweden in 1707 was really the father of modern botany and someone that Gilbert White often refers to. There were plenty of other books about growing things, one of the first on growing hops by Reginald Scot as early as 1574. White had a copy of Philip Miller's Garden Calendar of 1732, he was the curator of the Chelsea Physic Garden and Thomas Hitt produced a treatise of Fruit Trees in the 1780s, also there were plenty more of such works of practical advice.

Quite a different approach to the study of flowers was that of Mrs Delany who used them as subjects for delicate pictures made from paper together with exquisite embroidery; she was a friend of the Duchess of Portland after whom a number of sweet scented roses are named. All a rather refined approach to country pursuits.

Grimm's view of Selborne in 1776

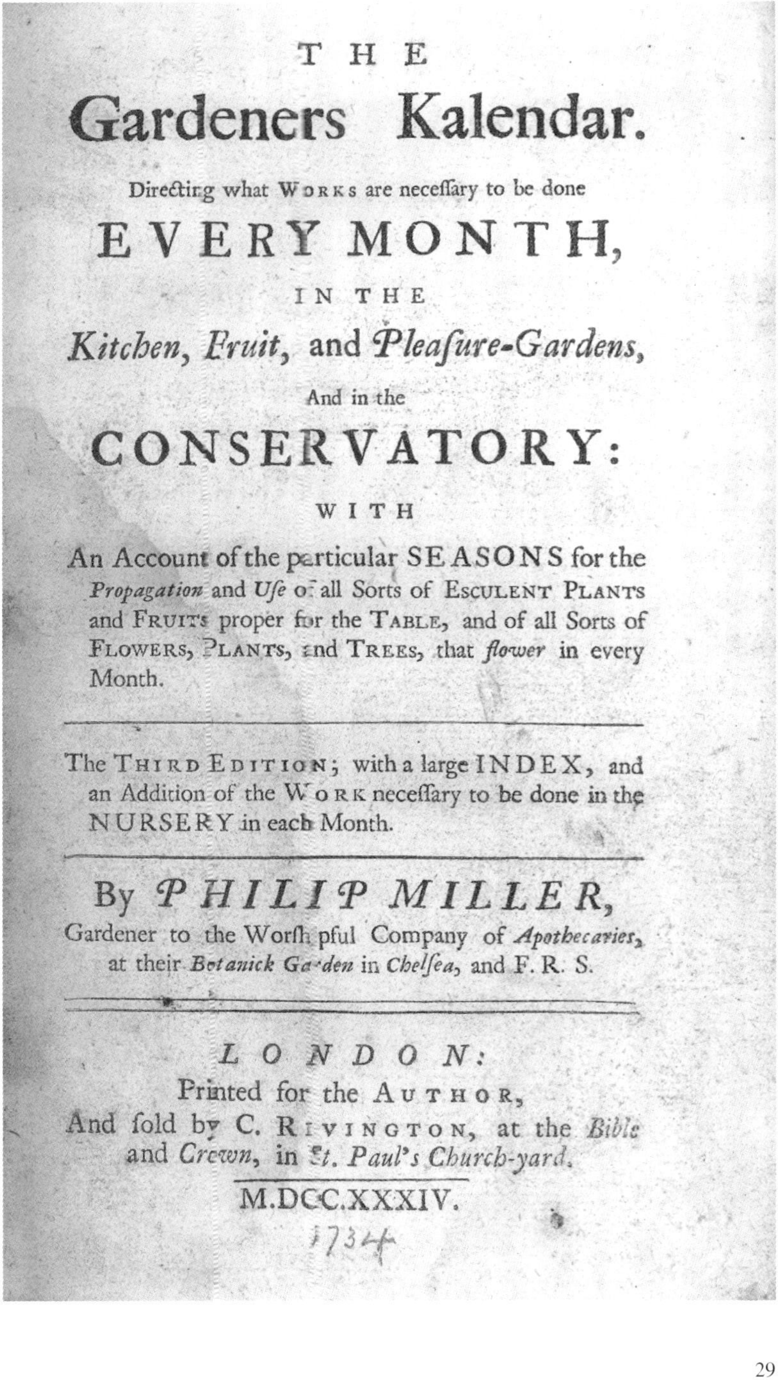

THE
Gardeners Kalendar.

Directing what WORKS are neceffary to be done

EVERY MONTH,

IN THE

Kitchen, Fruit, and Pleafure-Gardens,

And in the

CONSERVATORY:

WITH

An Account of the particular SEASONS for the
Propagation and Ufe of all Sorts of ESCULENT PLANTS
and FRUITS proper for the TABLE, and of all Sorts of
FLOWERS, PLANTS, and TREES, that *flower* in every
Month.

The THIRD EDITION; with a large INDEX, and
an Addition of the WORK neceffary to be done in the
NURSERY in each Month.

By PHILIP MILLER,

Gardener to the Worfhipful Company of *Apothecaries*,
at their *Botanick Garden* in *Chelfea*, and F. R. S.

LONDON:

Printed for the AUTHOR,
And fold by C. RIVINGTON, at the *Bible*
and *Crown*, in *St. Paul's Church-yard*.
M.DCC.XXXIV.

1734

But there were in the eighteenth century, those who wished to tame the countryside and yet contrive to make it naturalistic. These were the landscape gardeners and their results were called "le jardin anglais" to distinguish it from the styles of the continent.

Charles Bridgeman worked as Royal Gardener to George II and Queen Caroline, his best known work was the creation of the garden at Stowe in Buckinghamshire. More widely known is Capability Brown working from 1740s onwards. Taste was changing and Gilbert White when he moved into the Wakes in 1763 was undoubtedly influenced and had the Ha Ha built to bring the Hanger into uninterrupted view of the house, he was copying Brown on a much smaller scale. He and his brothers also made the Zig Zag path up to the top of the Hanger. Joseph Addison, a generation earlier, and after his Grand Tour to Italy had observed:

"A man might make a pretty landscape for his own possession"

Gilbert White travelled only in Southern England. As a boy he went to school in Basingstoke and as a young man to Oriel College, Oxford thus never becoming Vicar of Selborne which was in the gift of Magdalen College; hence he remained curate.

The writers of the eighteenth century confused us somewhat with their differing views of the countryside. For Gilbert White it was a laboratory for his keen observations of nature and for the delights of his garden expressed in the simple prose of his diaries and letters to Thomas Pennant and Daines Barrington both Fellows of the Royal Society. Oliver Goldsmith,

Selborne houses on the right and London houses of much the same period – 18th Century

almost his contemporary born in 1728, in Ireland, paints a dismal picture of the countryside in his poem "The Deserted Village" with somber words such as:

"And desolation saddenes all thy green" or

"Far far away thy children leave the land!!

Selborne did have its own deserted village at Hartley Manditt. On the other hand London attracted many writers, it was a growing city with fine houses in its new squares with nothing to compare in the village of Selborne. Samuel Johnson, the writer of the dictionary is so often quoted for his

"No Sir, when a man is tired of London, he is tired of life, for there is in London all that life can afford".

He felt no inclination to escape to the countryside. But Blake's poetry portrays a dreadful London of squallor and unhappiness and his phrase of

"Dark satanic mills" still haunts us with the worst effects of the Industrial Revolution which were never felt in rural Selborne.

William Wordsworth, born in 1770, and thus aged twenty three when Gilbert White died, claimed that he was "a worshipper of nature" (his own words) and saw the countryside, especially the Lake District, with a romantic vision linking his own inner feelings with the landscape. He went on writing poetry well into the next, nineteenth, century. But the countryside and villages like Selborne were not all idyllic delight – Thomas Gray's "Elergy" depicts a monotony of country life – the ploughman homeward plodding his weary way.

In 1784 Gilbert White notes in his Naturalists Journal that there was a riot on 7th April by villagers about being able to take wood fuel as part of their old manorial rights to the branches and tops of felled trees. Later was called the "Lop and Top Riot" in Holt forest to which the owner, Lord Stowell took exception.

At the end of the century prices were going up and that of the quartern loaf rose from $7^1/2^d$ to $12^1/2^d$ in London. Arthur Young, an eighteenth century commentator on rural affairs, in 1771 allowed for a man, his wife and three children the sum of 13 s 6d a week. By 1795 the suggested amount was 11s and 4d and early in the next century it had dropped to 8 s. Clearly causes for rural discontent were building up; so much for the village idyll.

We know something of day to day happenings in Selborne from accounts of the vestry meetings of the church. They show how much was spent on such items as the laundering of the church linen, buying the bread and wine for communion services and the repairing of prayer books. They show how the church building was kept in good repair, deciding to repair with wooden shingles made of cleft wood rather than slates because the latter were dearer.

There were also sums of money for killing of foxes and for destroying sparrows, the last occuring with great frequency. The bell-ringers had to be paid not only for the anniversary of Coronation Day but also to commemorate the Gunpowder Plot some one hundred and fifty years before.

A curious entry of the vestry meeting for 1724 was for the buying of tickets with charity money, for the State Lottery – they did not appear to have won anything. This was during the time when Gilbert White's grandfather, also named Gilbert, was vicar of Selborne. The Vestry also distributed clothing to the poor as well as beer to it's members.

The church building naturally occurs frequently in the Vestry Accounts – a gallery made of wood was built at the rear of the church in 1766 probably for the use of the church musicians and the children of Selborne School which Gilbert White (grandfather) had founded in the 1680s in accordance

ACM905.1.624

ACM905.1.624 Well Head Cottage – demolished for road widening in 1935

with the Church of England Society for the Propagation of Christian Knowledge.

Another entry records the purchase of 'reeds for the instruments'. There were frequent entries of a few pence for going to get things in Winchester which shows that Selborne was not culturally isolated and Gilbert White's visit to London, Bristol and of course Oxford as well as trips to the gardens at Blenheim and Stowe gave him a wide view of Southern England. His interest in antiquities took him to Stonehenge , all this on horseback for coach travel made him sick .

Gilbert White was not to see his book the Natural History and Antiquities of Selborne in the County of Southampton finally published by his brother Benjamin White, until 1789. It was an immediate success and soon went into many editions .

Thus the cult of the English Countryside was given a great boost from then on, with the name of the small village of Selborne being evocative of much that was best of the countryside in England.

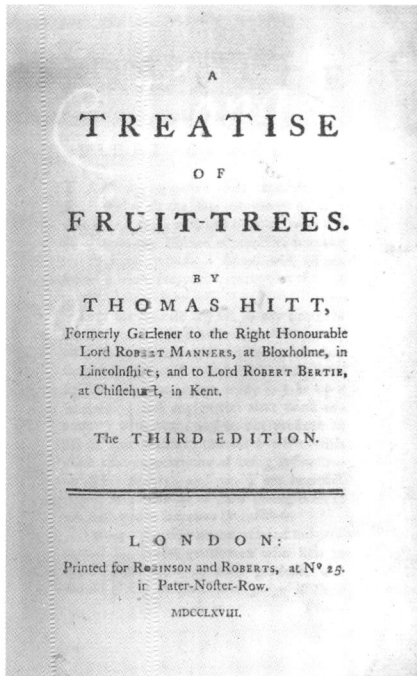

A

TREATISE

O F

FRUIT-TREES.

B Y

THOMAS HITT,

Formerly Gardener to the Right Honourable
Lord Robert Manners, at Bloxholme, in
Lincolnshire; and to Lord Robert Bertie,
at Chiflehurst, in Kent.

The THIRD EDITION.

LONDON:

Printed for Robinson and Roberts, at Nº 25.
in Pater-Noster-Row.

MDCCLXVIII.

Chapter 7

Queen Victoria's Century

Queen Victoria did not ascend the throne until 1837, she died in 1901 but much happened in Selborne before her time. It is possible to see trouble building-up among farm workers from the end of the eighteenth century. By the end of the Napoleonic war in 1815, the increasing use of machines in agriculture and reduction of wages led to riots among labourers in Wiltshire, Dorset and Hampshire under the name of an anonymous "Captain Swing". In our idyllic village of Selborne this manifested itself in a one day riot which became the subject of the folklore of the place, some of it based on real evidence and some on oral history. The front cover shows some attempt to reconstruct what happened. Several hundred peasants, perhaps we ought to call them farm workers, gathered in Selborne Monday 22nd November 1830. They first confronted the Vicar the Reverend William Cobbold to demand a reduction in tithes which were paid to him. He was clearly unsympathetic having experienced in the past angry Vestry Meetings about the part payment of wages under the Poor Law. The rioters, or mob as they were called, led by one John Newland with a trumpet – or was it a cow's horn? went on to attack the Poor House in Gracious street turning-out its inhabitants and setting fire to its furniture. The mob, or some of them, went on to Headley where there was already rioting and some men demanding food and money from the village shops. They ransacked the workhouse then went on to the next village Kingsley. The magistrates called in the military who made a number of arrests, Newland the trumpeter seems to have escaped. They were tried by special commissioners rather than magistrates in Winchester; the men were from various parts of Hampshire and two were publicly hanged. Others were sentenced to transportation to Tasmania and New South Wales mostly for their part in breaking the new agricultural machinery. Some of the Selborne men's descendants are living in Australia today.

The Selborne events were related verbally to W. H. Hudson about 1900 by his landlady whose father was the hornblower of the story. Our

cover illustrator has used the sketches of Robert Hills who lived from 1769 to 1844, for his ideas about the clothing worn by many farmworkers at this time. Whether a horn or a trumpet was blown on this occasion is of no historical significance.

There is a good deal of evidence about the state of the countryside during this period from the writings of William Cobbett. He lived from 1763 to 1835 part of the time at his farm at Botley so he knew Hampshire well including Selborne which he visited via Tisted, especially to see the village where "Mr White" had lived – the cult of Selborne was beginning to show. He describes Selborne as a "straggling irregular street bearing all the marks of great antiquity – I found here deep hollow ways with beds and sides of solid white stone". He mentions the yew tree in the churchyard, sadly no more, then, twenty three feet in circumference. He also saw and noted the hop fields around the village but suspected that the hops were infected with blight. He commented on the duty on hops at a penny to a pound of hops but doubted that it was collected. A Selborne boy showed him the way out of the village to Woolmer Forest and found the way excessively muddy with the wet 'malme' clay; he then went on to Headley. He had also noticed the grapevines around Selborne but wrote that they were badly pruned. He was impressd by the beauty of the area but suspected that the farmers and their workers were unhappy. Cobbett was a popular agitator and supporter of the "Labouring Classes" as he called them, but believed that many of them did not know how to brew their own beer or bake their own bread. Gilbert White clearly knew how to do all this and much more.

The increase in violence and pauperism after the end of the Napoleonic wars caused the government to pass the First Reform Bill in 1832 followed by the Poor Law Amendment two years later, which resulted in the gradual replacement of local poor houses with new workhouses supported by a "Union" of parishes. So Gracious Street Poor House was finally closed and Selborne poor had to be housed at the new Alton Union Workhouse.

In the late 1830s a great trade depression hit Great Britain and the United States of America with much unemployment especially in the new industrial cities, as well as many bankruptcies. Despite all this the great railway mania was in full swing although it was not until 1852 that the Guildford Farnham line was extended to Alton thus allowing access to

London by train. Conversely it meant that London people could easily visit Hampshire. The 1855 trade directory for Selborne tells us that letters received through Alton arrived at 9am and can be sent out at 4.30pm. The penny post had started in 1840 providing rapid communication to the outside world for villages such as Selborne.

Life in Selborne in the early nineteenth century could not have been all gloom and doom despite its riot. Jane Austen who lived at Chawton only a few miles away, wrote to her friend Cassandra that they should visit Selborne to go to the "gaieties" on its Common for the celebrations of King George III's birthday. The Reverend William Cobbold, involved in the roit, had died in 1841 and his place was taken by the Reverend Frederick Parsons, a Magdalen don, who rebuilt the old Vicarage. He hunted and rode all the week, had a great sense of humour and had an interest in birds and astronomy.

Gilbert White's old home, The Wakes, was occupied by members of the White family until 1844 when it was bought by Thomas Bell. He was a Fellow of the Royal Society and Professor of Zoology at King's College London and President of the Linnaean Society. Gilbert White's books had been printed in many editions and Bell was undoubtedly influenced to go and live in Selborne. The cult of the place was growing.

Selborne had never attracted a big house or mansion but in the 1860s a large estate was being created by the purchase of several farms in Blackmoor within the parish and to north of the village of Selborne. This estate was bought in 1865 by an eminent lawyer Sir Roundell Palmer who was Attorney-General in Lord Russell's government. In his youth Roundell Palmer had been a scholar at Winchester College so must have known the lushness of the Hampshire countryside. Latter in life Roundell became the first Earl of Selborne. One wonders if it was the association with Gilbert White's village, or perhaps the new railway at Alton, which persuaded him to buy this Blackmoor Estate – or just the right property at the right time? Soon he purchased extra farms at Oakwood, Sotherington and the Temple and became a landowner. He built a new church, vicarage, school and reading room at Blackmoor, commissioning an eminent Victorian architect Alfred Waterhouse to do the designs. The cult of the countryside was beginning to take a different form with Lord Selborne being concerned with the quality of life for the workers stemming from his High Church Anglicanism.

Later in the century agriculture was to suffer a serious decline partly due to the increased imports of grain from the United States and Canada. The Suez Canal had opened in 1870 and the introduction of refrigeration in ships brought large quantities of New Zealand lamb and dairy products to Britain. The trade directories for Selborne show that the number of farms and farmers greatly decreased between 1867 and 1903. The apple and fruit orchards at Blackmoor did not start until the 1920s. An interesting flashback to the middle ages shows a Selborne property paying a tithe of "apples, pears and nuts rather than the more common wheat, barley and hay".

The growing of hops in the Farnham, Alton and Selborne area was to alleviate some of the problems of agricultural depression. A harder blow to the country houses and estates was the introductions in the Budget of 1894 of death duties even on agricultural wealth and in 1909 the rate was increased when even rents were actually falling.

Then in 1914 came the Great War with even more disastrous effects on the countryside. Many estates went out of existence but Lord Selborne's estate survived and does today .

The magazine *"The Field"* had been founded in the middle of Victoria's reign and in 1897 another magazine, still being published, was called *Country Life.*

The Wakes had changed several times during this period, a Colonel Bibby had bought in 1910 and built or rebuilt the greenhouses growing exotic plants as well as re-designing the rose garden. He employed several gardeners and thus more work for local people.

Chapter 8

In and Out of Selborne

T he mediaeval lanes in and out of Selborne were tortuous and muddy in time became the sunken lanes we still have with us today. It was not until the 1750s that a "Turnpike road" was built from Alton to Winchester with a surface that allowed stagecoaches to travel rapidly from and to London. Gilbert White preferred to ride on horseback because he was coach sick; William Cobbett mostly used horseback but the poor still went on foot.

Alton was connnected to London by the railway via Farnham in1852 and there was soon another rail link when the Alton, Alresford and Winchester Railway was opened in 1865 .

The branch line through the Meon Valley had to wait until June 1903 after the passing of the London and South West (Meon Valley) Railway Bill by parliament some years previously. There was a station at Farringdon (sometimes spelt Faringdon) which handled mainly farm produce; there was another halt at East Tisted, which was only three miles from Selborne; the line then went on to Gosport. The steam locomotives had to change considerably over the previous half century and were now of a type easily recognised by older people today.

The Atalanta, 1859

Selborne people used the line especially to go to Alton's Tuesday market which was so popular that special market tickets were issued by way of Tisted price 7 pence (7d). They could also go to see the silent black and white films in the Alton Foresters' Hall. Buses were to come later in the 1920s but the Meon Valley line closed in 1955.

Adam's Tank of 1888

The motor car was beginning to appear at the turn of the cenury with a speed limit of 14 miles per hour in 1896 raised to 25 mph in 1903. Horse-drawn vehicles continued to be used extensively into the 1930s.

The bicycle, the safety bicycle with two similar sized wheels and pneumatic tyres was to make a considerable impact on country life; one could cycle to the nearest railway station and then travel all over Britain at 60 miles an hour or faster. The village of Selborne, with its memories of Gilbert White was a target for cycling clubs as well as individual young ladies.

Another result of the development of railways was the idea of railway time and because of the difference in sun time between London and Bristol, a standard railway time was introduced in 1845. Railway guards were provided with rather large but accurate pocket watches. The church clock in Selborne dates from the eighteenth century and had up to then had to be corrected by means of a sundial. In a letter of 1805 Jane Austen mentions a "compass and sundial in a shagreen case" which belonged to her father. A book called "The Young Man's Best Companion of the 1790s describes in some detail the mathematics of setting up a sundial.

The nearness of the railway was to allow the naturalist and writer, W H Hudson to visit Selborne on a number of occasions. Hudson, who was born in 1841, came to England in 1869 and soon was living in Bayswater in London from where he could escape to the countryside. He became entranced with Hampshire, especially with the New Forest and with Selborne. He published his book Hampshire Days in which he poured scorn on the urban collectors of butterflies and bird's eggs, hobbies which were popular at the that time. In this book he used the expression 'Selborne revisited' so he must have been there before. He mentioned two girls with bicycles at the foot of the zig-zag path with apparently vague ideas about Gilbert White.

Hudson stayed in Selborne in a thatched cottage opposite to the Queen's Arms in the days before motor cars made it dangerous to cross the road. The smell of the wood smoke from the blacksmith's shop a little further down the road would help him to remember the village. He visited Selborne for the third time, at least, in July 1901 noting that the birds had finished breeding and that the thermometer had reached the unprecedented high of 94 degrees!! He noted the sound of field crickets and the cirl buntings near the zig-zag suggesting he was more interested in nature than the topography of the countryside Gilbert White's Natural History must have been his constant companion.

Rather than the village itself, Hudson liked the common at the top of the Hanger and Nore Hill with its unkempt hedges which made it picturesque although indicating that farming was not at its best in the early years of the twentieth century.

He liked to visit a number of the village churches in the Selborne area noting, like White, that they were mostly "mean" and did not compare with the great wool churches of East Anglia and the Cotswolds. The Victorian church restorers or builders had done much work in Hampshire but Selborne Church was, more or less, not changed.

Hudson liked to talk to village people including his landlady who told him that her very aged mother's second husband was the celebrated trumpeter or horn blower who had rallied the mob to attack the Poor House in Gracious Street – a piece of history!

The fascination with the English countryside shows in another book, "The Cottage Book" which Sir Edward Grey began writing in 1894 at Itchen Abbas on the River Itchen halfway between Winchester and Alresford. It is mostly a diary account of all the birds and plants he saw

Farnham Road Cycling Club at Selborne c.1895

near his little weekend cottage. He and his wife Dorothy used bicycles to visit Selborne, Chawton and Alton. When he was Foreign Secretary he took Theodora Roosevelt, ex-president of the USA, for walks round Tichborne. The quietness of the Hampshire countryside and water meadows gave him relief from the cares of state.

The production of the cheap box Kodak camera in the 1890s gave many of the cyclists and other visitors the opportunity to take "snapshots of the countryside." The pictures postcard industry was to make pictures of Selborne available to it's many visitors who could post them with a halfpenny stamp to arrive anywhere in England usually within twenty four hours. They ended in the postcard albums which our grandparents treasured. In the trade directory of 1903 John Phillips Legg is shown as the sub-postmaster, his father having been Selborne's carpenter, builder, undertaker, saddler and harness maker; trade tended to be dominated by a few families such as the Leggs and the Maxwells.

STONE-CURLEW

Common in Selborne in Gilbert White's time but no longer

41

Chapter 9

Hops

The growing of hops in the Selborne area warrants it's own chapter. Flemish weavers had brought hops to England in the reign of Edward III but their use did not become established and in Tudor times it became regarded as a "pernicious weed ". However tastes do change and ale became less popular and hops had to be imported to flavour beer, an everyday drink until the introduction of tea in the eighteenth century.

Kent was the main county for growing hops followed by the Farnham, Alton and Selborne, although William Cobbett visiting Selborne in 1823 said that "they were of poor quality". The fields where they were grown were called hop gardens, mostly about twelve acres in size. The plants were supported by poles and grew to a height of twenty feet; the plants lasted for several years and the poles were cut from coppice wood.

"hop poles on the ground £45"

in an inventory of 1678 .

The picking of the flowers needed a great deal of labour, more than could be supplied by the farm-workers or villagers so that large numbers of towns people were recruited as temporary pickers. The influx every summer of large numbers of families from London and towns such as Portsmouth was a feature of life in this part of Hampshire, right up to middle years of the twentieth century when hop growing declined and stopped.

For the pickers, this annual "holiday" in the countryside was a change from their built-up and smoky town environment to one of clean air and greenery. Some of the hop pickers lived in tents and some in sheds provided by the farmers. A number were gipsies who lived in their horse-drawn caravans some of which were of the old "bow top" type with a green canvas cover. Later ones were of the box shape with windows which glowed when the oil lamps were alight reflected in the Ruby Glass which was often collected. Lord Selborne provided them with fire-wood for

Hop gardens at Selborne c.1920

their cooking fires. Generally the gipsy families were accepted by the local people and their children went to the village school listed as "travellers". They were not always welcomed in the public houses whether they were gipsies or Londoners because of the bad language and fights! The hop picking usually started at the end of August or September.

The families picked the flowers into large sacks called "pockets" which had the date and the name of the farm stamped on them. In Hampshire the sacks had a large bell emblem showing that the contents were of first quality, two bells meant second quality. Often the same families came to the same farm each year. Each picker or family had a card with the dates and the number of bushels they had picked and finally how much they were paid by the bailiff or talleyman. By 1930s this was between 3 1/2d and 9d per bushel. They often seem to have spent the money buying new clothes and shoes for the winter, but some spent it in the pub!

Local people participated too and the effects of this show in the School Log Books with children involved with many agricultural activities as well as hops. Here is a selection of Selborne school entries

1887	18th July	many children who have been absent for haymaking have now returned to school 111 present this morning
1888	13th August	choir outing to Brighton
	17th august	six weeks holiday for harvest and hop-picking
1889	28th June	low attendance for haymaking
	6th August	closed school for harvest and hopping
1893	8th Nov.	Viscount Wolmer (son of Earl Selborne) visited school and presented a map of the British Empire and a Union Jack

Slightly fewer entries for the war years and no mention of Armistice Day 11th November 1918

Another log book Selborne C/E school 1st 1926 to October 1943

1936	23rd Sept.	School opening was postponed till Sept.28th because of late hop-picking.
1938	8th Aug.	installation of electric light and a note by one of His Majesty's Inspectors of schools referring to this in 'Gilbert White's village.'
1939		no mention of war starting but 36% of village children away hop-picking.
1940	13th August	at 7 o'clock German planes dropped six bombs which fell near New Barnes Road.
1944		no mention of "D" day
	18th May	List of old boys killed in war
		Henry Cannings – North Africa (Army)
		Will Rushton – East Indies (Navy)
		Two brothers Phillips – one Iraq one Navy
		Norman Hayward – Normandy (Army)
	24th August	out break of Scarlet fever so school closed by Medical Officer of Health

Then follows a poignant personal note by the Headmaster:

"My son (an old pupil) David Dagwell reported missing. He dropped with the 1st Airborne Division at Arnhem. This is to record the fact with my pride, admiration and hope"

With relief he was reported a prisoner of war on 11th November 1944.

The Father of the present 4th Earl of Selborne was killed on active service while serving with the Hampshire Regiment.

After the war the log book still records hop-picking right up to the 1950s but by 1970 there is no mention of absences for hop-picking or harvesting; smaller amounts of hops were now grown and a hop-picking machine was now available; post war women were now working regularly and in any case went to holiday camps like Butlins for their holidays, which they could now afford.

Chapter 10

The Cult of the Countryside

I n the nineteenth century many people left their villages to work in the expanding industrial cities which were swallowing much of the countryside. London was expanding in all directions with suburbs reached by the many railways and electric tramways. It was apparent that people were losing their roots.

John Ruskin, not a country dweller, was to draw attention to the idea that life was more than the accumulation of money; he was looking at the qualities which the world of art and architecture ought to provide. It was his contact with Octavia Hill, a social reformer, and later with Canon Rawsley, that a group of middle class intellectuals were to form what was to become the National Trust, finally founded in 1895

"to preserve places of historic intrest or natural beauty permanently for the nation to enjoy".

But it was not untill 1932 that parts of Selborne were to be donated to the National Trust by Magdalen College Oxford whose ownership dated from the time of the closure of the priory in the fifteenth century. It consisted

Oxen ploughing, Norton Farm, Selborne 1900

of two hundred and forty acres, mostly beechwood on the Hanger forming Selborne Hill and common. A few years later Mr R. Edgar of Newton Valence Place donated another twenty acres of the Short and Long Lythes, all to be enjoyed by the villagers and the visitors.

A few years before the foundation of the National Trust the Society for the preservation of Ancient Buildings was started under the guidance of William Morris.

The act of Parliament allowing enclosures of the old open fields at Selborne was as late as 1866 whereas much of Farringdon had been enclosed as early as 1749. Fields with hedges as we know them often date from that time. Yet a photograph of John Waterman's farm at Norton in 1900 shows ploughing with two teams of oxen, six animals in each, a method little changed from the middle ages.

Some of the postcards available were reproductions of the paintings of popular artists such as Myles Burket Foster and Helen Allingham showing an idealised

countryside with thatched cottages surrounded with flowers and with pretty children standing by the gate. Some country cottages may have been like that but many were not. None at the end of this Victorian period had electricity or gas, few had any sewage systems – only earth privies at the bottom of the garden. Very few had a mains water supply, relying on a well with a bucket and chain; sometimes with a pump. Selborne had several good constant springs and wells. The first Lord Selborne was to build several model cottages on the Blackmoor Estate but they had to rely on paraffin oil and candles as a means of lighting. The village of Selborne in the early years of the twentieth century, the Edwardian Era, was still a very self-contained place. The many visitors would have noticed the prosperous looking grocers shop belonging to Maxwell and Sons; they had been in the village for over half a century and were provision merchants, drapers, bakers, wine and spirit merchants. There was also a Post Office owned by John Legg which was also a drapers and grocers, as well as a general stores selling ironmongery and tobacco. The Post Office was important, for in 1909 the Government introduced Old Age Pensions for those aged 70 and over. It was only five shillings a week or 7s6d for married couples but helped to avoid the shadow of the dreaded Workhouse. There was also a butcher's shop, a boot and shoemaker, a saddler, a blacksmith and a wheelwright who was also the undertaker. The visitors could have got refreshments at the Queens Arms whose proprietor was a Mrs Jane Brickell, or at another public house The White Hart.

Horse-drawn vehicles in use in the early 20th century

The population of Selborne at the beginning of the twentieth century (1901) was 1,430 and it seems to have been a generally healthy place with numbers of people living into their eighties and a few into their nineties. There still continued to be clusters of infant and child deaths although not so many as in the middle years of the nineteenth century. The Trade Directory for Selborne for 1920 still shows the Maxwells as grocers and John Philips Legg at the Post Office and that by 1911, the population had reached 2,118, But what it does not show is that the Great War 1914-18, now called the First World War, had resulted in seventeen young men being killed including the Hon. Robert Palmer, son of the 2nd Earl of Selborne who was killed in action in Mesopotania which we call Iraq. Also killed this time in France, at Arras in 1917, was Edward Thomas the poet who lived at Yewtree Cottage at Steep within walking distance of Selborne. he and his wife Helen went by footpath. His poetry reflects his love of the English countryside, of its birds and flowers and even its green "Nettles" made all the more beautiful in contrast to the horror of war all around him. Although born in Lambeth in London the pull of the countryside was too strong for him to remain there and so he became more of a countryman than many who were born on farms or villages. When we read Edward Thomas' poems, with the knowledge of his untimely death, we may feel intense love for the countryside for ever under attack by the modern world, with its destructive wars and vastly increased populations.

Chapter 11

Memory

T he final chapter takes us to the edge or limit of memory, if not for the reader, then for his or her parents. The twentieth century changes in many respects after the Great War in 1918 although the school log book shows the continuation of the rural heritage with harvest and crop growing.

In the 1920s and 30s change came quickly and fundamentally. The increasing use of the motor car saw more and more invasions of the countryside including Selborne. The railways had already brought newspapers on the day of publication to all the villages and in 1922 came 2LO, soon to become the BBC; First came crystal sets and then battery operated sets whose accumulators needed recharging at the local garage. This brought news, national and world-wide to town and as well as the country with a national language rather than country dialects.

The spread of houses to the suburbs and ribbon development along new roads, saw semi-detached housing being built some with mock Tudor facades. Selborne got its share of early twentieth century villas and now some exceutive style houses whose occupants commute daily to some place of work which is not Selborne.

Between the two wars, the years 1918 to 1939, there were many books written about the countryside for the ordinary reader, or perhaps for the owner of a motor car, motor cycle or for the energetic cyclist. H V Morton's "In Search of England" is one of the earliest books followed in the 1930s by the many books published by Batsford Ltd with authors such as Adrian Bell and Edmund Blunder with Gilbert White's Selborne in many of them. Between the wars The Wakes was still in private ownership.

Tractors, first imported from USA during World War I were beginning to take the place of farm horses and Kelly's Trade Directory for Selborne 1930 shows only one blacksmith and one wheelwright. It does however

ACM905.1.147

ACM905.1.147 The main Street looking towards Alton
– The Selborne Arms is on the left – 1937 still horses and bicycles

show Ronald Waterman as an agricultral engineer. In the 1939 directory the blacksmith is Mrs Alice Tarr presumably the widow of the 1930 entry, but there are now two motor engineers, Leslie Coles and Herbert Maltby.

Then, in September 1939 came the beginning of the second world War with its rationing of food and clothing, its blackout and air raids and, of course, casualties. It brought conscription of young men into the armed forces and some young women too. The love of the English countryside had a great appeal to men in the deserts of North Africa or the jungles of India and Burma even though most of the men had lived all their lives in towns and cities. A nostalgic song with the words "– when you come home again –" rhymes with the image of a "country lane", eleven from Selborne never did come home! The author found himself reading Thomas Hardy, Mary Webb and Henry Williamson in remote and dismal places and the National History of Selborne could be found on the shelves of bookshops in the bazaars of India. In 1943 John Arlott who lived in Alresford, selected poems in an anthology, county by county, called Landmarks devoted to the countryside. Under Hampshire he chose Gilbert White's "The Invitation to Selborne, which begins

"Oft on some evening sunny, soft and still".
The anthology was reprinted in 1988 under the title The Coloured Counties taking a line from A E Housman's poem Bredon Hill, he had died in 1936 before the war.

It was not until after the war period that people woke up to the fact that Gilbert White's house ought to be preserved and made available for people to see and enjoy. So in 1953 The Wakes was purchased with help from the Oates family and became a museum. It is now part of the village scene with its adjacent thatched cottage and behind it the Great Mead, the meadow between this house and the foot of the Hanger, as well as the area where Gilbert White had his beloved garden.

Later a Field Study Centre was to be added, now in a transplanted barn close to the foot of the zig-zag path. Large numbers of school children come to study at the centre learning much about natural history. Their coaches are part of the increased traffic so that the once quiet village street now experiences traffic jams.

The British Sunday has been eroded in this modern world so pubs and shops are open every day and all day. The pace of life is much faster leaving little time for quiet reflection or contemplation. The visitors have driven home before the nightingale starts singing, if indeed it ever does now. The wireless of the 1930s attempt to capture something of the English countryside by broadcasting the song of a nightingale from a Surrey wood, sadly not the same as the real song. No one sees a glowworm while riding in their car nor would they hear the skylark which is now rarely

ACM905.1.602 Recapturing the past.
Mr Legg(?) leading with shepherd's crook – 20 July 1938

heard even by the walker. Hops are no longer grown but one farmer is now growing lavender instead.

In 2002 and 2003 Selborne like other southern villages is faced with the possibility of being included in a South Downs National Park the boundaries of which have not yet been decided. The prospect has generated much controversy among those who might be included. One of the aims of the Park would be countryside conservation of most of the South Downs and the Hampshire Hangers, but allowing more access by people who live outside the area.

Selborne, with Gilbert White's writings, has undoubtedly played its part in planting a seed of the Cult of the Countryside which we, now, in the 21st century must cultivate with great care.

NIGHTJAR

Appendix A:

AGE	NEOLITHIC	BRONZE AGE	IRON AGE	ROMAN BRITAIN	DARK AGE	ANGLO SAXON	MIDDLE AGES (Medieval)	RENAIS- SANCE	INDUSTRIAL REVOLTION
(dates)	2000 1500 1000	500	BC 0 AD	500	1000	1500	2000		
VISIBLE REMAINS	Longbarrows	Roundbarrows (Tumuli) Stonehenge	Hillforts Dykes Earthworks	Roads Villa foundations Town walls Baths Forts Hadrian's Wall	A few churches Decorated bibles Boundary banks		Castles Cathedrals Abbeys Monasteries Parish churches Gothic centuries	Great houses Timber houses	Factories Windmills Cottages Town houses Mansions Canals Railways Bridges
NAMES	Personal and Tribal names in Britain all lost and forgotten so we use these names to describe these long periods of our pre-history: Neolithic Age — First simple farming tools of stone, bone, wood. Bronze Age — Farming - tools and weapons of bronze. Iron Age — Farming and exporting food, tools and weapons of iron.		Names of local Kings and Chiefs from coins. / Tribes, people and towns from early writers. / Some river and place names survive from Celtic centuries.	Roman names from tombstones. Emperors' names from coins.	Names of towns and villages survive but few personal names.		Names of Kings and Queens, clergy, nobles, merchants, from: Domesday Book 1086 Charters Pipe Rolls Family letters	Our surnames have been in use from this time. / From 1538 Parish registers give names from baptisms, marriages and burials (from 1837 kept in Somerset House) / The first useful census in 1851	
EVENTS	Prehistoric Britain / Knowledge of which is gained almost entirely by archaeology and aerial photography.			55BC Julius Caesar visits Britain / 43AD Romans under Claudius conquer Britain / 410 Romans leave Britain	597 St Augustine brings Christianity to England / 878 - 900 Alfred's reign	1066 Norman conquest of England / 1086 Domesday Book / 1096 - 1270 Crusades / 1215 Magna Carta / 1349 Black Death - plague / 1346 - 1453 Hundred Years War with France	1455 - 1485 Wars of the Roses / 1536 Henry VIII closes monasteries / 1564 - 1616 Shakespeare / 1642 - 1648 Civil War - cavaliers & roundheads. The King against Parliament	1776 Declaration of American Independence / 1825 First Railway / 1837 - 1901 Queen Victoria / 19?? You were born

Appendix B:

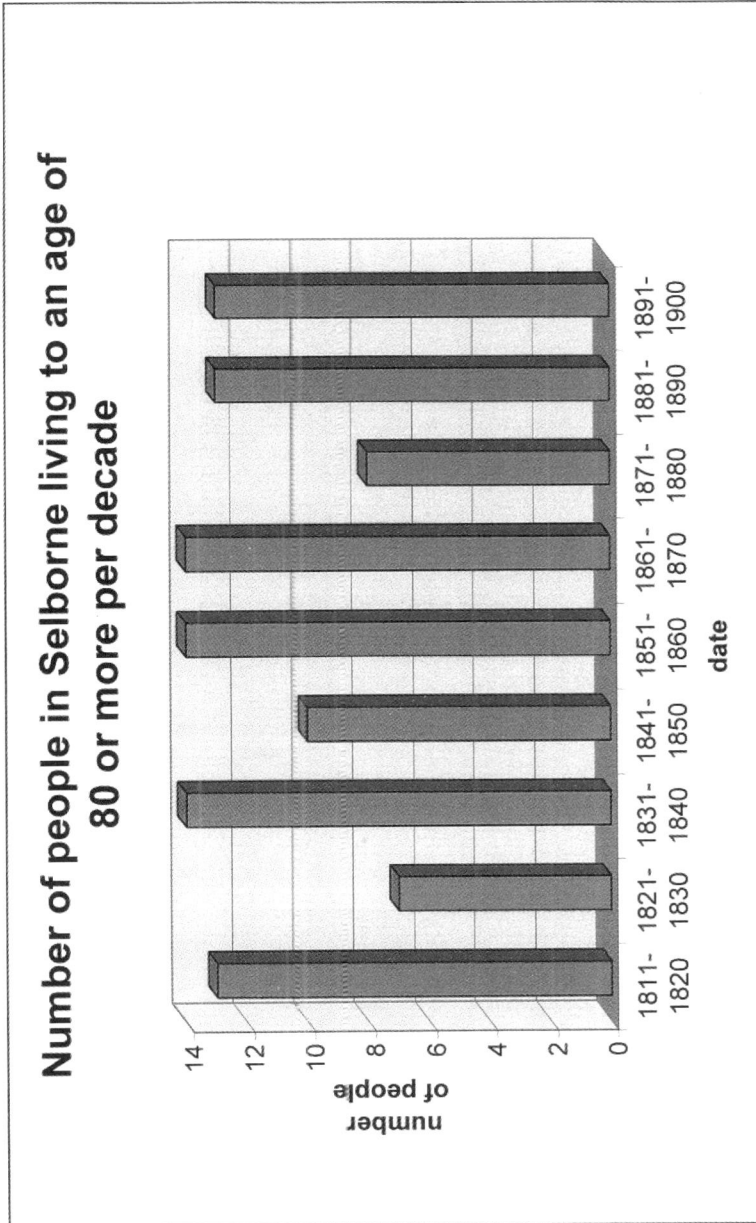

Number of people in Selborne living to an age of 80 or more per decade

Appendix C:

Medical Research Council 1925, Table VII: Percentage increase in population

Increase	1861	1871	1881
Urban %	17.58	17.57	19.37
Rural %	1.43	2.96	1.17

Appendix D:

Since metrication in Britain was adopted, many readers may
not know, or have forgotten the following tables

Money

$^{1}/_{4}$ penny	=	1 farthing
12 pence	=	1 shilling
20 shillings	=	1 pound
21 shillings	=	1 guinea

Older coins and denominations

4d	=	1 groat
2s	=	1 florin
2s 6d	=	half crown
5s	=	1 crown
6s 8d	=	1 noble
13s 4d	=	1 mark

Weight

16 ounces	=	1 pound (lb)
14 pounds	=	1 stone
4 stones	=	1 quarter
4 quarters	=	1 hundredweight (cwt)
20 hundredweight	=	1 ton

Length

12 inches	=	1 foot
3 feet	=	1 yard
22 yards	=	1 chain
10 chains	=	1 furlong
8 furlongs	=	1 mile

Liquid or capacity

4 gills	=	1 pint
2 pints	=	1 quart
4 quarts	=	1 gallon
2 gallons	=	1 peck
4 pecks	=	1 bushel

Square or Area

144 square inches	=	1 square foot
9 square feet	=	1 square yard
$30^1/_4$ square yards	=	1 square rod, pole or perch
40 perches	=	1 rood
4 roods	=	1 acre
640 acres	=	1 square mile

Modern measurements

5 acres	=	2 hectares

Bibliography

The Victoria County History Hampshire Vol 3

Hampshire Treasures (Archaeology)

Hampshire Field Club Vol 30 – 1973 Selborne Priory
by Deirdre le Faye

Selborne Association Newsletters – various articles
by Dr. E. M. Yates

Blackmoor and its people (A celebration of the Millennium)

Gilbert White – The Natural History of Selborne (Everyman)

Gilbert White – The Antiquities of Selborne in the County of
Southampton ed Sidney Scott 1950

Gilbert White's Year – pages from the Garden Kalendar
and the Naturalist's Journal 1751 - 1793
sel. by John Commander (Scholar Press) 1979

Gilbert Whites – A Selborne Year ed E. Dadswell and Nicola Armstrong

Mabey Richard – Gilbert White a biography 1986

Austen Jane – Letters My Dear Cassandra ed. P Huges – Hallet (Collin
and Brown 1990)

Doherty J. – Ancient Lanes and Tracks (Hampshire Countryside
Heritage 1981)

Godwin G. – The Civil War in Hampshire 1904

Grey Edward – The Cottage Book republished Victor Gallanz 1999

Hudson W. H. – Hampshire Days 1903

Platt Colin – Medieval England, a Social History and Archaeology from
the Conquest to 1600 (Roytledge and Kegan Paul 1978)

Southern R. W. – Western Society and the Church in the Middle Ages
(Penguin 1970)

Index